Star Friends

Enchanted Mist

To the very talented designers Sophie Bransby
and Kat Cassidy who make all the Star Friends
books look so wonderful! – LC
To Robyn for all her support – KB

LITTLE TIGER
An imprint of Little Tiger Press Limited
1 Coda Studios, 189 Munster Road, London SW6 6AW

Imported into the EEA by Penguin Random House Ireland,
Morrison Chambers, 32 Nassau Street, Dublin D02 YH68

A paperback original
First published in Great Britain in 2023

Text copyright © Linda Chapman, 2023
Illustrations © Kim Barnes, 2023

ISBN: 978-1-78895-626-0

A CIP catalogue record for this book is available from the British Library.

Printed and bound in the UK.

The Forest Stewardship Council® (FSC®) is a global, not-for-profit organization
dedicated to the promotion of responsible forest management worldwide. FSC
defines standards based on agreed principles for responsible forest stewardship
that are supported by environmental, social, and economic stakeholders.
To learn more, visit www.fsc.org

FSC
www.fsc.org

MIX
Paper | Supporting
responsible forestry
FSC® C171272

2 4 6 8 10 9 7 5 3 1

Star Friends

Enchanted Mist

Linda Chapman
Illustrated By Kim Barnes

LITTLE TIGER

LONDON

In the Star World

A snowy owl with silver feathers swooped silently through the forest and came to land on the edge of a rocky pool with a mirror-like surface. The branches of the tall trees around the pool reached up to the star-filled sky, their leaves and trunks glittering. There was a faint rustle as three more animals appeared out of the shadows — a stag, a wolf and a badger. Their fur was tipped with silver and their expressions were wise.

"It appears our four young Star Animals

and their Star Friends from Westcombe have managed to stop magic from causing chaos again," said Hunter the owl, sweeping one wing over the pool. An image of a campfire surrounded by children and adults appeared on the surface. A little way off, nestled against some trees, four girls were cuddling four animals — a young fox, a fallow deer, a red squirrel and a wildcat with a tabby coat. The animals all had indigo eyes just like the wolf, the stag, the badger and the owl. Everyone looked very happy.

"They did well," the wolf said softly. "It helps that they have such a strong friendship."

The others nodded.

"They worked together and stopped people getting hurt," said the stag.

"But they haven't yet realized that there is another Star Animal close by," said Hunter.

The picture changed to show a sleek brown otter with sparkling indigo eyes.

"Fen is inexperienced with Star Magic and needs to learn more. Her Star Friend must also learn not to use other forms of magic unwisely. I hope our young friends will be able to help."

"They need to find Fen first," said the badger.

"Let's hope they do before the magic causes more problems," said the stag.

"Shall we see what happens when they return to Westcombe?" said the wolf.

The others nodded and they all settled down to watch.

CHAPTER ONE

Maia tossed and turned in her sleep. Her
dreams were filled with images: her school
in Westcombe; an otter bounding towards a
person with long dark hair; a kitchen counter
with cooking equipment; a group of girls from
her school shouting angrily at each other...

The images changed into memories of the
holiday she had got back from a week ago.
She saw a smouldering campfire with shocked
campers standing round it and a clearing
littered with branches from destroyed dens...

Maia woke and sat up in bed, pushing her dark blond fringe out of her eyes. Glancing at her alarm clock, she saw that it was only five thirty, too early to get up for school. Bracken was curled up by her feet. He raised his head. "Maia? Are you all right?"

Bracken was a fox from the Star World. When they first met, he had told her how young animals from his home came to the human world to find a Star Friend – a child who believed in magic and who liked helping people. Being a Star Friend involved learning how to use magic to make the world a better place and, when a Star Animal bonded with their Star Friend, they stayed with them their whole life.

Bracken had taught Maia how to connect to the magic current that linked the two worlds, and Maia had discovered she had the ability to use a mirror or other shiny surfaces to look into the past and future and see what was happening elsewhere. Soon after Maia had met Bracken, her friends Ionie, Sita and Lottie had also become Star Friends. They could do other things with the current, and they all worked together to stop anyone causing trouble using magic. Maia thought it was amazing being able to do magic with her best friends and their animals!

Bracken wriggled up the bed and snuggled next to her. "You look worried."

Maia rubbed her forehead. "I was having a really vivid dream."

"Was it a magic dream?" Bracken asked her.

Maia's dreams sometimes showed her things she and her friends needed to know to protect other people.

"Maybe. There was a load of stuff at the beginning that didn't seem to make much sense, and my magic dreams are often like that."

Maia told him what she'd seen.

"It could mean trouble might be coming to Westcombe," said Bracken. "We'd better tell the others."

"We're going to the clearing after school," said Maia. "We can discuss it properly then."

The clearing was in the woods near Ionie's house. The girls often went there because it was a beautiful place of very powerful magic. Hardly anyone else ever visited the clearing, which meant it was a safe place where they could practise magic with their animals.

Although they all went to school together, they had to be careful not to talk too much about magic in case anyone overheard. The animals had told them that Star Magic had to be kept completely secret.

"In my dream, I also saw stuff that happened when we were camping," Maia told Bracken. "Things the Jeniyan Spirit did."

On the first day of their camping holiday, Miss Amadi, one of the adult helpers and Maia and Ionie's new class teacher, had tried to comfort Ionie, who was feeling nervous. She'd offered to lend Ionie her lucky wooden monkey, putting him into her hands and telling her that he would look after her. The teacher hadn't known that the monkey contained a helpful Jeniyan Spirit or that the touch of Ionie's Star Magic could wake it up. When the Jeniyan Spirit came to life, it had set out on a mission to make sure Ionie had a good time at camp. Unfortunately this had also put everyone else in danger.

"I'm glad you stopped the spirit before it

hurt someone," said Bracken.

Maia nodded. "Do you remember we thought that all the bad things that were happening in camp were because of Mrs Coates, the farmer from next door?"

"She was very grumpy," said Bracken. "Well, until the final night."

Something about that had been niggling at Maia ever since. "That was a bit weird, wasn't it? Mrs Coates went from being *un*friendly when we arrived to being *really* friendly on the last night." She voiced the thought she'd been having since camp. "You don't think she changed because of magic, do you?"

Bracken looked surprised. "You mean you think the Jeniyan Spirit had something to do with her change of heart?"

"No," said Maia, remembering how the spirit had told them it didn't know Mrs Coates. "Not that. I was thinking that there might have been some other magic going on at camp – maybe the raccoon ornament that someone left at Mrs Coates's house was magic."

A small garden raccoon ornament had mysteriously turned up in Mrs Coates's porch on the day the camp had started, although no one admitted to having put it there. The raccoon held a pink crystal acorn in its front paws engraved with the words: *I bring the gift of friendship*. Ever since she'd seen the crystal, Maia had wondered whether it was magic. She and the others had encountered magic crystals before and knew just how powerful they could be.

"You might be able to find out more using your magic," Bracken said.

A smile caught at Maia's mouth. "OK." She never turned down the chance to do magic!

She picked up the pocket mirror that was on her bedside table and flipped open the lid. Taking a deep breath, she let her mind connect to the magic current and felt it flowing into her, making her body warm and tingly. She smiled as she remembered how hard she and the others had found doing magic at first. Now it was almost as easy as breathing.

"Show me anything magic that happened at camp," Maia whispered to the mirror.

Her reflection faded as the surface swirled with light and then a picture appeared: a collection of ornaments on top of a wooden crate covered with a scarf. Among them was the carved wooden monkey with a smiley face that had contained the Jeniyan Spirit.

"What about any other magic?" Maia asked.

The image flickered, briefly showing her

an otter on the bank of a stream. Maia frowned. She'd seen an otter in her dreams, too. Weird. Why was she seeing one now? But then the picture changed again, revealing a raccoon holding a pink crystal acorn in its front paws.

"It's showing me the raccoon ornament!" Maia said excitedly, forgetting about the otter. The crystal acorn sparkled brightly. "I bet I'm right and the crystal is magic – some kind of good magic that makes people friendly."

"Show me who left the raccoon in Mrs Coates's porch," she said eagerly to the mirror. She held her breath as the surface of the mirror revealed a slim figure with dark hair in a ponytail hurrying up the farmhouse path towards the porch.

"It was a girl or a woman with long dark hair, but that's all I can see," she told Bracken as the image faded.

"Maybe we'll never know who it was," said Bracken. "There were lots of people at camp, people you won't see again, but if the magic was doing good I think we don't need to worry about it. We only have to stop bad things happening when someone uses magic."

Maia nodded. He was right, even though she couldn't stand the feeling that there was a mystery she hadn't solved. It was like getting to the end of a jigsaw puzzle and realizing there was one piece missing!

Bracken nuzzled her neck with his cold black nose. "Let's concentrate on the things your dream showed you about Westcombe. The magic could be trying to tell you that there's something we need to watch out for."

Maia hugged him. "If something bad is about to happen, we'll find out and stop it!"

Chapter Two

It was a beautiful early summer day and, as
Maia walked to school with her mum and her
little brother Alfie in his buggy, she thought
how pretty Westcombe looked. Gardens and
window boxes were spilling over with bright
flowers, and lawns were neatly mown. Around
the edges of the recreation ground red poppies
were nodding their heads in the long grass,
and in the duck pond on the village green
there were little brown-and-yellow ducklings
paddling behind their mother.

While Alfie talked happily to the blue toy train he was holding, Maia and her mum chatted.

"I can't believe that soon we're not going to be walking to school together," Mrs Greene said. "You'll be getting the bus with Clio and heading off to King John's."

Maia had been at the village primary school since she was four. She was excited at the thought of starting at the secondary school where her older sister Clio went, but also a bit nervous, too. She'd been there for a visit and it seemed so big! She was sure she was going to get lost or forget the teachers' names.

"It'll be weird not seeing everyone from my class every day," she said.

Although a lot of people from her year were going to King John's, some, like Lottie, were going to different schools.

"You'll make new friends," said her mum.

Maia nodded. Ionie, Lottie and Sita would always be her best friends but she was definitely planning on making new ones, too.

"And now, for the rest of this term, you can really enjoy the time you've got left together," Mrs Greene went on. "Your teachers have got lots of fun things planned, haven't they?"

"Yep. This week it's Super Science Week and we have sports day on Thursday," Maia said.

She always enjoyed sports day, and Super Science Week sounded good, too. They were going to do all sorts of stuff like make ice cream without a freezer, launch rockets, mix perfumes, have competitions and build a working torch – it sounded loads more fun than their usual science lessons!

When they got to school, the playground was already filling up. While the parents, grandparents and childminders chatted, the younger children ran round the field and climbed on the play equipment. The older ones played football or stood around, talking in groups. Maia saw Lottie, Ionie and Sita sitting on the wall at the far side of the playground. "I'll see you later," she said to her mum and Alfie.

"I'll pick you up from Ionie's at seven," said Mrs Greene.

"Yep – bye!" said Maia.

"Maia! Thomas!" shouted Alfie, waving his train at her.

Maia grinned. "Sorry. Bye, Thomas!" she said

seriously, blowing a kiss to Alfie's train. Alfie beamed and she hurried off to join her friends.

As she made her way through the crowds, a tall girl with long dark brown hair held back by two sparkly silver slides smiled at her. "Hi, Maia."

"Hi, Maddie," Maia said, pausing.

Maddie was in her class. She had only started at the school at the beginning of the Easter term and she hadn't made many friends yet. She'd got on well with the girls she'd shared a tent with at camp, but they were all in the other Year Six class. "Are you looking forward to Super Science Week?" Maddie asked.

Maia glanced to where Ionie, Sita and Lottie were sitting. She really wanted to tell them about the dream she'd had, but she didn't want to be unfriendly. "Yeah. It sounds fun."

Maddie gave her a shy look. "If we need to have a partner, can we team up?"

Maia hesitated. She usually paired up with Ionie.

"It's OK – it doesn't matter," Maddie said when Maia didn't reply straight away.

"No, I'd really like to," Maia said quickly. "It's just I usually go with Ionie." She saw the disappointment on Maddie's face. "But maybe we can be a three?"

Maddie's eyes lit up. "I'd like that!"

"Maia!" Ionie shouted, waving.

"Over here!" called Lottie.

"I'd better go. See you," said Maia.

Maddie smiled and waved as Maia ran off to join the others.

"We thought you were never coming over,"

Ionie said impatiently. "We've got something important to tell you." She dropped her voice. "Lottie had one of her weird feelings this morning."

"One of my magic feelings," whispered Lottie, tucking a strand of curly hair behind her ear. "The ones I get when something bad is going to happen."

"Really?" Maia replied. "I had an odd dream – I think it was a magic one warning me about something."

"Were there any Shades in it?" breathed Sita, her brown eyes wide. Shades were evil spirits who came from the shadows.

"No, just school, someone's bedroom, a kitchen and a group of people arguing," Maia said. "Oh, and a person with an otter."

"An otter?" echoed Ionie.

Maia nodded. "I don't know why I saw an—" She was interrupted by the sound of the bell ringing – the signal for them all to get in line and go to their classrooms.

"We can talk more after school when we go to the clearing tonight," Ionie said quickly, tightening her strawberry-blond ponytail. "We definitely need to work out what's going on."

Maia's tummy fizzed with excitement. She loved it when they had a new mystery to solve!

☆★☆

Maia and Ionie were in a different Year Six class to Sita and Lottie. Their teacher was Miss Amadi. She had taken over a week ago when their usual teacher, Miss Harris, had left to have a baby. Maia and Ionie both liked Miss Amadi. She was fun and told really interesting stories about her aunt and cousins who lived in Nigeria and what she'd seen and done when she'd travelled round the world before she started teaching. She had been one of the adult helpers on the camping holiday and always wore colourful clothes to school. Today her long braided hair was tied back with a brightly patterned headscarf.

"As you know, it's Super Science Week so most of our lessons will involve science," Miss Amadi told them once she had taken the register. "You'll also be practising for sports day. Your first practice session will be after break, but we're going to start with a science lesson all about smells!"

She explained how essential oils could be extracted from plant leaves or seeds or the rind of fruit such as oranges.

"Essential oils have been used for centuries, and they all have different properties. Some, like lavender, make you feel relaxed; others, like rosemary, make you feel full of energy." Miss Amadi's eyes shone enthusiastically. "They can do so many things!"

Ionie put her hand up. "How do you get oil out of a plant?"

"There are several different ways but today

I'm going to show you how to use a process called distillation," Miss Amadi said, indicating a collection of flasks and tubes on her desk. "I'll demonstrate how that works, and then we'll have a smelling competition to see if you can guess which plants the different oils have come from. After that, you can all make your own bath oil or – for those who are feeling ambitious – your own perfume!"

Miss Amadi used a copper still to get the oil from mint leaves, showing the class how steam from boiling water rose through the plant leaves, extracting the essential oil, which was then collected in a flask.

"You don't need an expensive still like this though," she explained. "I have a slow cooker at home that I use when I'm extracting essential oils." She smiled. "But do ask your parents' permission! Now it's time for our smelling competition. Let's see who's got the best nose in the class!"

Chapter Three

Miss Amadi put a tray of fifteen little brown bottles on every table, each one labelled with a number. The class had to smell them and guess the plant they came from. Ionie was very pleased when she got the most right answers – she was very competitive and loved winning.

After the smelling competition, Maia and Ionie went over to one of the perfume tables together and started to follow the instructions on the sheets there. Maia was smelling the different oils they could use when Maddie joined them.

"Can I work with you?" she asked.

"Sure," said Maia.

Ionie didn't answer. She was too busy counting out the exact number of drops of jojoba oil the instructions said to start with.

Maia and Maddie chatted as they smelled the oils and wrote down a shortlist of their favourites.

"I like your ruler," said Maia, noticing that there were pictures of otters on it. It reminded Maia of the otter she'd seen in her dream.

"Thanks. I love otters – they're so cute," said Maddie. She smiled. "I love all animals."

"Me too," said Maia.

"Horses are my favourite. Do you go riding?" Maddie asked.

Maia shook her head.

"I used to go every week before we moved," said Maddie, "but my mum's been too busy to find a new riding school for me. She said she will in the holidays though." She pushed her dark hair back behind her ears. "I can't wait to start again."

Just then Miss Amadi came over. "How are you all getting on?"

"Good," said Ionie, holding up a little brown bottle she had been carefully filling with drops of oil. "I've put eighty drops of jojoba, ten bergamot, five drops of lemon and five drops of basil in mine."

"Excellent choice," said Miss Amadi. "That should be a very energizing oil."

"Can I have a look at the still now I've finished?" Ionie asked.

"Of course, but please don't touch it because there's boiling water inside," said Miss Amadi.

Ionie nodded and went over to where the still was. "How about you two?" Miss Amadi asked Maia and Maddie.

"We haven't started making our perfumes yet," Maia admitted.

"There are so many oils to choose from!" said Maddie. "I don't know which ones to pick."

"OK, well, let's see if I can help. What do you want the perfume to do? Do you want to be relaxed, creative, calm, happy…?"

"Popular?" said Maddie hopefully.

Miss Amadi smiled. "I'm afraid a perfume can't do that, Maddie."

"I wish something could," Maddie blurted out. Then she blushed, looking as if she wished she hadn't spoken.

Maia felt sorry for her. It couldn't be easy starting a new school two-thirds of the way through Year Six when everyone was already in firm friendship groups.

Miss Amadi put her hand on Maddie's arm.

"It's not easy being new at school, is it?" she said sympathetically. "When I was growing up, I moved around a lot because of my father's job, so I know just what it's like to have to start over and make friends. I'm sure it'll soon get better."

Maddie nodded slowly, her blush fading. She smiled at Miss Amadi. "Thanks, Miss," she said, sounding happier.

"Right, let's get you both some oils," Miss Amadi said. "I'll choose a few and you can select the ones you like best."

After smelling some that Miss Amadi had suggested, Maddie and Maia both decided that they wanted an oil that would make them feel happy. They chose rosemary, lavender, grapefruit and geranium, although Maia used a few more drops of the lavender and Maddie added a few more drops of the grapefruit oil.

They mixed the oils together in the quantities that Miss Amadi told them.

"Now you just need to put the lids on, shake the bottles and write your names on them," said Miss Amadi, nodding to some little brown labels on string that they could tie round the bottlenecks.

While Miss Amadi went to help another table, Maia and Maddie labelled their perfumes and put some on their wrists. They were almost the same scent, only very slightly different.

⭒★⭒

"That was the best science lesson ever," said Maia at breaktime as she and Ionie went outside.

"It was," said Ionie. "It was cool seeing how the still worked." She lowered her voice. "I wonder if people who do plant magic have to distil the essence of plants and herbs."

Maia shrugged. "I don't know. Maybe."

"I wish we knew more about different kinds of magic," said Ionie longingly. "We've learned about Star Magic and how to use that but we really don't know much about the other kinds out there like plant magic and crystal magic, and there's probably other kinds of magic, too. When I'm older, I'm going to try to find out more about every kind."

Maia nodded. She thought it was interesting but she didn't have the same urge to understand things that Ionie had. She was happy just using Star Magic. That was amazing enough!

As she looked round the playground for Sita and Lottie, she noticed Maddie sitting by herself on a bench.

"Maddie's on her own," she said, nudging Ionie. "Should we go and talk to her?"

Ionie spoke quietly. "If we do, we won't be able to discuss magic."

"We can do that after school," said Maia, remembering Miss Amadi and Maddie's conversation about how hard it was to make new friends if you moved school. "Let's go over and talk to her."

Maddie seemed really pleased when they sat down next to her. Sita and Lottie looked a bit surprised when they came out of their classroom, but they soon joined the three girls. They talked about which schools they'd be going to in September and found out that Maddie would be at the same one as Lottie.

As Maddie and Lottie talked about the clubs they wanted to join – they both wanted to be in the pet club and the environment club – Maia felt pleased they'd come to talk to Maddie. She knew Lottie was a bit worried about going to a new school without the rest of them. If she and Maddie got on, then maybe that would make both of them happier.

After break, the whole of Year Six had

a sports day practice. Nick, the sports coach, told them about the events. Some were serious, like sprinting and high jump and throwing – they all had to take part in those – but there were also going to be some fun events like an obstacle race, an egg-and-spoon race, a balancing-a-beanbag-on-your-head race and a sack race that they could do in teams. The team that got the most points in each year group would win a prize.

"First things first: I need you all to get into teams of three or four," Nick said. "In the teams of three, someone will have to go twice in each event."

Maia, Lottie, Ionie and Sita quickly grabbed each other. They were definitely going to be a team!

Maia saw Maddie standing by herself. "Can we be a team of five?" she asked Nick.

"No, sorry, Maia – four is the maximum," he said.

Maia felt awful when no one picked Maddie.

Nick told Maddie to join up with a group of three boys. She walked over to them slowly. Glancing across the playground, Maia saw Miss Amadi watching from the classroom window. A little while later, she saw the teacher leaving the building and hurrying out through the school gates.

"Where do you think Miss Amadi's going?" Maia said to Ionie.

Ionie shrugged. "I think she lives near school. Maybe she's going home because she's not feeling well or to pick up something she's forgotten."

When they went back to the classroom after getting changed, Maia was relieved to see that Miss Amadi was back and looking OK. She had put a big ball of sticky Blu-tack, a roll of

Sellotape and some packs of paper straws on each table and was inspecting the bottles of perfume and bath oil the class had made.

"Some of these smell great," she said, screwing the top back on a bottle. "This is my favourite, I think." She looked at the label. "Maddie, it looks like you made this one. Why don't you let people smell it?"

Maddie took the bottle Miss Amadi was holding out and rolled some on to her wrists.

"That's really nice," said Sadie, who was standing next to her.

"Yeah, I like it more than mine," said her friend Tara.

"It's so zingy and fresh," added Ionie, sniffing.

"Mmm," said Amy, who was close by. "I wish that was mine."

Maddie looked thrilled.

"You can take your perfumes and bath oils home later, but now we're going to have an engineering competition. Let's see which group can make the longest bridge using just the things on your tables." Miss Amadi clapped her hands. "Time to get started!"

☆★☆

Maia thought that it was one of the most fun days she'd ever had at school. After they finished their bridges, they went outside and made chocolate ice cream using ice and salt to freeze a mixture of cream and chocolate milkshake powder that was in a separate bag. Maia was delighted when Ionie asked Maddie if she wanted to work with them. Even better, when they all tasted each other's ice cream, quite a few people said they thought Maia, Ionie and Maddie's was the best.

Afterwards, they sat on the grass and ate their ice cream while Miss Amadi explained the science behind the ice-cream experiment. It was all to do with the salt making the temperature of the ice drop. Maia didn't really understand, but Ionie asked lots of questions.

"If we didn't have magic to practise, I almost wouldn't want school to end today," Ionie whispered to Maia when they were heading back into the classroom.

"Magic?" said Maddie.

Maia swung round and saw that she was right behind them.

"What are you talking about?" Maddie said curiously.

"Um…" Maia swapped looks with Ionie, wondering what to say. "I … um…"

"Conjuring magic!" said Ionie quickly. "After school, we're going to practise some conjuring tricks. We're putting on a magic show for our parents."

"Oh," Maddie said, looking a little disappointed.

"Did you think we meant real magic?" Ionie asked curiously.

Maddie looked flustered. "Um … no … of course not!"

"Hey, Maddie," said Tara, joining them,
"I like your hairslides."

"Yeah, they're cool," said Sadie, overhearing.
"Where did you get them?"

They left Maddie talking to Tara and Sadie
and hurried inside.

"Phew! That was close!" Maia whispered to
Ionie.

Ionie grinned at her. "So are you ready to
do some conjuring then?"

Maia felt a sharp surge of excitement at the
thought of doing magic with her friends and
their Star Animals. "Definitely!" she replied.

Chapter Four

After leaving their bags at Ionie's house, Maia,
Lottie, Sita and Ionie headed to the stony
lane that ran all the way from Ionie's house
on the main road, down a hill to a shingle
beach. There was a pretty thatched cottage
halfway down the lane where Maia's Granny
Anne used to live. She'd died almost a year
ago, and Maia still missed her. She'd discovered
that her granny had also been a Star Friend
– her animal had been a beautiful silver wolf.
Knowing that comforted Maia but she did

wish that she'd been able to talk to her about being a Star Friend, and that her grandmother could have met Bracken.

A new family had recently moved into Granny Anne's cottage – two men and their little boy who had started at the same playgroup as Maia's brother, Alfie. One of the dads was pushing the boy on a swing in the garden. Maia waved as they passed and the two of them waved back.

Opposite the cottage there was an overgrown footpath. The girls pushed their way through the tall green stalks and heavy white heads of cow parsley and jumped over the brambles that snagged at their ankles. The air was heavy with the smells of summer – blossom, green leaves and damp soil. They reached the end of the overgrown path and stepped out into a quiet, sunny clearing.

Butterflies fluttered around in the still air, honeybees buzzed in and out of the wildflowers and a clear stream gurgled and tinkled as it flowed down a small waterfall of rocks and disappeared into the trees on the far side of the clearing. Maia had first met Bracken in this clearing, and he had told her it was a particularly magical place.

She was just about to call Bracken's name when she noticed the branches of a blackberry bush on the other side of the clearing moving. She peered more closely and saw an animal watching them from the shadows. She caught her breath, remembering the animal she'd seen in her dream. "Look!" she whispered to the others. "It's an otter!" But even as she pointed at the bush, she realized she was wrong. The animal looked similar to an otter but its dark brown coat was fluffier, its ears pointier and its face was paler around its eyes and muzzle.

"It's not an otter, it's a polecat," whispered Ionie. "They're really rare."

The polecat backed further into the shadows and disappeared.

They all smiled at each other. They loved it when they caught sight of wild animals in the woods.

"Let's call our animals," said Sita.

"Bracken!"

"Sorrel!"

"Juniper!"

"Willow!"

There was a swirl of starry light before the four Star Animals appeared.

Bracken leaped up at Maia, his indigo eyes shining with happiness at seeing her again. Juniper, the red squirrel, jumped on to Lottie's shoulder, playing with her curls and chattering softly in her ear. Willow, the fallow deer, nuzzled Sita's face with her nose while Sorrel, the tabby wildcat, pressed herself against Ionie's legs and purred.

Maia hugged Bracken. "I've missed you," she said.

"And I've missed you. Are you going to tell everyone about your dream?"

"I told them a bit about it at school. We can talk more later. I want to do some magic first!" she said.

Her friends seemed to have the same idea. They could each do different things with the Star Magic. When Lottie connected to the magic current, she became incredibly agile and fast. Now she set off at a run and threw herself into a series of perfect handsprings and somersaults before climbing swiftly up a tree with Juniper beside her and then swinging from a branch.

Meanwhile Ionie transformed herself so she looked just like Miss Amadi with braided hair caught back in a thick ponytail and a bright scarf around her neck. She could use the magic to cast glamours, which meant she could disguise herself to look like someone else. She could also travel from place to place, using shadows, and she was a Spirit Speaker, which meant she could send spirits back to the realms they came from.

Maia had her seeing magic, and she could also conjure magic barriers. She opened her mind and felt the magic surge into her. Shutting her eyes, she imagined a protective bubble all round her. "Try to hit me with something!" she called to Lottie.

Lottie dropped down lightly to the grass and picked up some pine cones. She threw them at Maia but they bounced off the invisible shield that Maia had conjured.

"That's brilliant, Maia!" said Bracken, prancing around in excitement and accidentally jumping on Sorrel's tail.

The cat hissed indignantly at him.

"Whoops! Sorry, Sorrel!" Bracken said.

Sorrel glared at him. "Clumsy creature!"

"Grumpy cat!" Bracken retorted cheekily.

"Bracken, why don't you see if you can get through my barrier?" Maia called quickly, not wanting him and Sorrel to start bickering. "You could—"

She was interrupted by Sita. "Hey, everyone! Come here!"

She and Willow were standing by the stream. The things Sita could do with magic weren't quite as easy to practise – she could calm people down, heal injuries, and she could command people or magic spirits to do whatever she wanted. She found that power quite scary though, so only ever used it in an emergency.

"What is it?" asked Maia.

"Willow can smell another Star Animal by the stream," said Sita.

The others heard and ran over.

"I can smell it, too," said Sorrel, sniffing along the rocks. "The scent is faint but another Star Animal has definitely been near the water."

"Does that mean there's another Star Friend in Westcombe?" Lottie said.

"Possibly, but it's more likely a young Star Animal who hasn't found their Star Friend yet," said Sorrel.

Juniper nodded. "If someone was connecting to the magic current, we'd all sense it. Our fur tingles when someone uses Star Magic nearby, and I haven't felt anything."

"Actually, I did feel a flicker of something today," said Willow. "But then it passed. I thought I'd imagined it."

"I definitely haven't felt anything," said Bracken.

"I wonder what kind of animal it is," said Sita.

"I think I might know!" Maia said excitedly. "I saw an otter in my dream last night and again when I asked the magic to show me anything that had been magical at camp."

"Oh wow! So there could be a Star Otter looking for its Star Friend?" breathed Sita.

"Wait," said Ionie. "The camp was an hour away by car. Why would the otter be in those woods and now here?"

They all considered it.

"Maybe there are two Star Otters?" Maia suggested, though even she had to admit it didn't seem very likely.

"Or," Lottie said excitedly, "maybe the otter was at camp, and it made a Star Friend there. Someone who lives in Westcombe. So now it's travelled here with them."

"Ooh yes, that could be it," said Juniper, jumping from Lottie's left shoulder to her right.

"And if it's only just met its Star Friend then that could explain why they haven't started using the magic current yet," said Sorrel.

"Which is why we haven't felt anyone using Star Magic!" said Bracken, waving his bushy tail.

"We should try to find it," said Willow. "It might not know how to teach its new friend to use the magic current."

Juniper nodded. "We were lucky. We all had each other, and we helped one another. It would have been much harder if we hadn't had friends."

Maia pulled her compact mirror out of her pocket – she always took it with her wherever she went. She never knew when she might need it to do some magic! "I'll see if I can find anything out with this."

She sat down on a rock and, with Bracken cuddling up to her side, she opened her mind to the magic current. "Show me if a Star Otter has been here in the clearing," she breathed.

A thrill ran through her as an otter appeared in the mirror, swimming in the stream. It had sleek brown fur, a white chest and a cheeky look on its face. Its sparkling eyes were a deep indigo.

"We're right – there is a Star Otter," Maia told the others. "Show me where it is," she said to the mirror.

The image of the otter vanished, replaced by a street in Westcombe. There were houses and cottages along both sides of a long road with a brook running through the centre of it which was lined with weeping willow trees.

Maia recognized
the street straight
away. "It's
showing me
Brook Street," she
said. "By school."
"Do you think that
means the otter's Star Friend
lives somewhere on that
street?" said Sita.

Maia gave a strangled
squeak. "Maddie lives on
Brook Street! I've seen her
coming out of a house
there. It's just opposite the
road that goes up to school."

"Maybe she's the otter's Star Friend," Sita
said excitedly.

"She was at camp with us," said Lottie. "She
could have met the otter there."

Maia remembered something else. "When

she overheard Ionie and me talking about magic earlier, I asked her if she thought we were talking about real magic and she looked all flustered."

"Do you think she could be a Star Friend?" said Sita.

Maia felt a wave of excitement sweep over her. "We have to find out!"

Chapter Five

Maia tried asking the magic to show her Maddie with the otter, but nothing appeared on the surface of the mirror. So she asked it what Maddie was doing.

A picture of Maddie appeared. She was sitting on her bed with a laptop open on her knees and a notepad beside her. Maia noticed some posters of animals on her bedroom walls. One of them made her eyes widen.

"She's got a poster of an otter," she told the others excitedly. "And, at school, she had a ruler with otters on!" She was feeling more and more convinced that they were right – Maddie must have met the otter at camp and was now a Star Friend!

As Maia watched, Maddie got up from the bed and put the laptop on her bedside table. Maia caught a glimpse of the screen and saw a website. There were some strange symbols across the top and the words:

So you want people
to like you?
This is what to do...

Maia suddenly felt uncomfortable. She was sure Maddie wouldn't want her to know she'd been looking at a website about making friends. She shut the mirror and let her connection to the current fade.

"I didn't see the otter so I don't know for sure if Maddie is its Star Friend," she said. "But I don't want to keep watching her. It feels wrong."

"We have to find out if she's a Star Friend!" said Ionie.

"I know but Maia's right – we shouldn't watch Maddie without her knowing," said Sita. "I wouldn't like it if someone did that to me."

Lottie nodded. "Let's try to think of another way to get proof."

"And then, when we do find out, we can tell her we know," said Maia.

"But only when we're absolutely sure," said Sorrel. "You absolutely must not tell her about Star Magic until you know she's a Star Friend."

"We'll wait until we're certain," Maia agreed.

☆★☆

That night, Maia's dreams were full of vivid images again. She saw the otter gambolling in the clearing in the woods, starlight glittering round it. She saw it cuddled up in someone's arms. The person had dark hair but her face was buried in the otter's fur. She saw Maddie in her bedroom, sitting at her desk and reading out something from her laptop that was open. It was surrounded by a jumble of objects – books, the perfume bottle from school, a hairbrush, some lip balm and a bottle of water. While she said the words, Maddie moved one hand in the air, almost as if she was drawing pictures with her finger…

☆★☆

Maia woke up when her alarm went off.
She rubbed her eyes and yawned. When she
dreamed a lot, she always woke feeling as if she
hadn't been to sleep. She was sure the dreams
were magic dreams but she didn't know why
it was important that she should see Maddie
in her bedroom. What had she been doing
drawing strange shapes in the air with her
finger? Why had the magic shown Maia that?
She gave her head a shake, trying to clear it. At
the end of her bed, Bracken was snoozing in a
doughnut shape, his nose touching his tail.

Maia leaned over and kissed his forehead. He opened one eye and then stretched lazily, rolling on to his back. She tickled his downy tummy, and he snuffled at her neck with his nose, tickling her and making her giggle. "Oh, Bracken, I love you so much," she said, cuddling him.

His eyes shone as he snuggled closer. "I love you, too. I'm very glad you're my Star Friend."

Maia's heart swelled happily.

Just then her phone buzzed. It was a text from Ionie.

> I think I've had an idea how to find out if Maddie is a SF!

It was followed by a row of excited emojis. Maia texted back.

> How?

> I'll tell you later 😉

> Tell me now!

Ionie just sent her a row of laughing faces in reply.

Maia sighed. She knew there was no point asking Ionie any more. Ionie could be really annoying when she had an idea, but wasn't ready to share it.

"Maia! Are you up?" her dad called from the landing.

"I'm up!" she called back, giving Bracken a last kiss and getting out of bed.

⭐⭐⭐

Maia was just walking past Maddie's house when Maddie came out of the front door.

"Hi." Maia let her mum and Alfie go on and waited for Maddie to join her. It felt a bit weird seeing her after they'd been talking about her the day before.

"I wonder what we'll do in science today," said Maddie as they crossed the road together. "Yesterday was fun. I love my perfume, and making the ice cream was brilliant. I hope we do some good things today, too." She took her perfume out of her pocket and rolled some on her wrists.

"Yeah," Maia agreed. She got a waft of Maddie's perfume. It did smell good. She took her own bottle of perfume out from her bag and dabbed it on to her wrists. It was almost the same. "If we're in groups, shall we work together again – you, me and Ionie?"

Maddie looked pleased. "Yes, let's."

Maia felt a sudden rush of warmth. Maddie was so nice. *If she is a Star Friend, then she'll be able to be a proper part of our friendship group*, she thought. *Oh, I really hope she is!*

Maia's mum had stopped to talk to another mum. "I'll see you after school," she said to Maia as Maia and Maddie reached her and Alfie in his buggy.

"Bye," Maia said.

Alfie waved his train at her.

"Bye, Thomas!" Maia said.

"I like your train," Maddie said to Alfie.

Alfie studied her for a moment and then gave her a beaming smile. "Me like you!" he declared.

Maia looked at him in surprise. He was usually quite shy with people he didn't know.

Maddie giggled. "Your little brother is so cute," she said to Maia as they joined the throng of people going through the school gate. Sadie and Tara were just in front of them. After a few moments, they both looked round.

"Hey, Maddie!" said Sadie.

"Do you like my hairslide?" Tara asked, showing her the glittery slide she was wearing. It was similar to the one Maddie had been wearing the day before.

"It's really nice," said Maddie.

"We're thinking of going shopping on Saturday. Would you like to come with us?" Sadie said.

"I'd love to!" said Maddie, looking delighted. "What time are you going?"

The three of them walked off together. Maia felt a bit put out. She was pleased for Maddie that Tara and Sadie were being friendly but she'd been hoping Maddie would come and chat to Ionie, Sita and Lottie with her.

"Maia!" Maia glanced round as Lottie ran to join her. "Did you get a text from Ionie this morning?"

"About her idea?" said Maia.

Lottie nodded. "She wouldn't say what it was."

"She wouldn't tell me either," said Maia,

pushing thoughts of Maddie away. "What do you think it is?"

"I haven't a clue but knowing Ionie it'll be good," said Lottie. "Let's go and see."

Ionie was sitting on the wall with Sita.

Maia ran over. "So come on!" she urged, sitting down beside her. "What's your big idea?"

"Yes, please tell us," Lottie begged. "*Please*."

Ionie looked at them, a teasing glint in her eyes. "It's probably best to wait until after school…"

"No, we want to know now!" they all chorused.

Ionie gave in with a grin. "OK." Her voice dropped to a whisper. "Well, my idea is —" she paused dramatically — "Psychic Susan!"

"Who?" Maia frowned.

Sita gave a gasp. "That's the fortune-teller you disguised yourself as when you went to the Psychic Fair, isn't it?"

"Yep!" said Ionie. "When the cakes in the

café were being charmed with magic, and everyone wanted to eat them."

"That was such a weird feeling," said Maia, remembering the way she'd craved those cakes. She hadn't been able to think about anything else!

"My plan is to disguise myself as Psychic Susan and call at Maddie's house when we know she's home," said Ionie. "When she answers the door, I'll talk to her about magic and see if she gives any clues that she knows it's real. What do you think?"

Maia grinned. It was a typical Ionie plan. Slightly crazy but brilliant. "It's a great idea!"

"As long as you don't get into any trouble," said Lottie anxiously.

"I won't," said Ionie airily.

"When are you going to do it?" Sita asked.

"Tonight, after school!" Ionie's eyes shone. "Get ready for some fun!"

CHAPTER SIX

In class that morning, they made bath bombs
with bicarbonate of soda and watched how
they fizzed away when placed in water. Maddie
worked with Maia and Ionie on them. Maia
hoped they'd spend break time together,
too, but Tara and Sadie came over to talk to
Maddie, and she went off with them. Maia
saw Miss Amadi smile as she watched the three
girls leaving the classroom together. She looked
happy to see Maddie making friends at last.

It is good Maddie's making friends, Maia

thought, feeling a slight prickle of jealousy. *But I wanted her to hang around with us! I'm sure she likes us better than Tara and Sadie.*

Maia sat with Ionie, Sita and Lottie on the wall as usual but, while Lottie told them about an argument between two people in her gymnastics group, Maia found herself looking round to see where Maddie was.

"Maia, are you even listening to me?" Lottie said in frustration, breaking off.

"What? Course I am," said Maia, dragging her eyes away from the field where she had spotted Maddie sitting with Tara and Sadie. Three of the boys – Brad, Tyler and Jake – had gone over and were talking to them, too.

"What's so interesting over there?" said Sita curiously.

"Nothing. I was just wondering what Maddie was doing," said Maia.

"We should ask her to have lunch with us," Ionie said.

Maia nodded. "Definitely. She's lonely – she hasn't got any friends," she explained to Lottie and Sita.

Lottie glanced across at the field. "Really? It looks like she's getting on pretty well with Tara and Sadie and the boys."

"But she likes us better," said Ionie quickly. "I know she does."

Maia lowered her voice. "And we may find out she's a Star Friend. Let's have lunch with her. Please!"

Maia saw Lottie and Sita give each other

puzzled looks, but then they shrugged. "OK then," said Lottie. "If you want to."

After break, the two Year Six classes came together for sports day practice. Amy, Lucy and Shruti from Maia's class ran over to Maddie at the start and asked her if she wanted to join their team. Maddie seemed to really enjoy being with them. At the end of the practice, she went into the lunch hall with them, talking happily about ponies. Maia felt strangely grumpy. She'd really wanted Maddie to sit with her and the others.

For a moment, she wondered why it mattered so much. Why did she keep thinking about Maddie all the time? She frowned. A memory tugged at the corners of her mind of a time when she'd felt like this before…

But then it slipped out of reach and, with one last look in Maddie's direction, she sighed and went to find her friends.

☆★☆

"I can't believe you're really going to do this, Ionie," Lottie said as they hid in the branches of one of the weeping willow trees by the brook after school. The branches curved down round them, like a green tent, hiding them from the rest of the world. "What if something goes wrong?"

Ionie had disguised herself as an old woman with a long red skirt and a black shawl round her shoulders. Her grey hair was pulled back into a bun, and her face was wrinkled. Only her eyes still looked like Ionie's – green and sparkling with excitement.

"I don't know what you're talking about, my dear," she said in a wheezing voice. "Nothing will go wrong."

"What if your disguise fails, and Maddie sees the real you, or her mum answers the door, and you don't get to speak to Maddie?" said Lottie.

"Poof!" said Ionie, waving a hand. "My disguises never fail, and Maia's going to watch with her magic and tell me when Maddie's mum looks like she's busy doing something. Then I'll knock on the door."

"I am?" said Maia.

Ionie nodded firmly. "You are."

"OK." Maia got her mirror out. "Show me Maddie's mum," she said. The surface of the mirror swirled and she saw a picture of a dark-haired woman sitting on a sofa, talking on the phone while Maddie sat next to her, reading something on her laptop. "Now might be a good time," Maia said, and she told Ionie what Maddie and her mum were doing.

"OK, here goes then," said Ionie. "Sorrel!" she called. The wildcat appeared beside her. "It's time."

"You're taking Sorrel!" Sita said in surprise.

"Of course. I want her to see if she can smell the otter," said Ionie.

"But people don't just walk around with cats!" said Sita.

"Psychic Susan does," Ionie said, and before Sita or Lottie could say anything more she pushed through the curtain of willow leaves and crossed the road towards Maddie's house with Sorrel trotting at her heels, her tail high in the air. They looked a very strange pair.

"Oh, I hope she's going to be OK," said Sita, peering out from between the leaves with Lottie.

"This really is a risky idea," said Lottie anxiously. "Something's bound to go wrong."

Maia looked into the mirror. "Show me Ionie," she said, and Ionie appeared in the mirror. Maia watched as she shuffled across

the road and up to Maddie's front door.
She pressed the doorbell. A few moments
passed and then the door opened.

"It's Maddie!" Lottie hissed excitedly.

Sita gripped her arm.

Maia watched Maddie eagerly. "Let me
hear what's being said," she said, pulling the
mirror closer to her ear.

"Um … hello," she
heard Maddie say
uncertainly.

"Hello, my
pretty," Ionie said
in her wheezing
voice.

Sorrel started
sniffing at the
driveway.

"Can … can I
help you?" Maddie
asked Ionie.

"Or maybe I can help you, my dear – with the power of magic!" Ionie declared.

"Magic?" echoed Maddie.

"Yes, MAGIC!" Ionie rolled the word out. Maia grinned. She could tell Ionie was loving being in disguise. "Psychic Susan can see into the future." Ionie waved her hands wildly in front of Maddie's eyes. "Psychic Susan can see into the past! Psychic Susan can sense you know the truth about magic, my dear!"

Maddie leaned forward. "I do. I know magic's real," she whispered. "Spells and stuff do work, don't they?"

Maia caught her breath.

"Yes! Spells. Potions. Charms," Ionie said eagerly. "Crystals. Plants. Stars…"

Maia studied Maddie's face. She was looking confused. "I don't know about some of those things but…"

"Maddie?" Her mum appeared behind her. Seeing Ionie, she frowned. "Who are you?"

"I am Psychic Susan!" said Ionie dramatically. "Teller of fortunes. Seller of magic. And … and…" Her eyes fell on Sorrel. "Trainer of cats!"

Maia started to giggle as she saw the look of astonishment on Maddie's mum's face.

"What's going on?" said Lottie, looking round. She and Sita were too far away to be able to hear what was being said on the doorstep.

"Ionie's just told Maddie's mum she trains cats," said Maia.

"She what?" said Sita.

"Shh!" Maia said, concentrating on the mirror.

"Well, I'm afraid we don't want any magic or fortunes told here, and we don't have any cats," said Maddie's mum. "So please could you leave now?"

"Very well," said Ionie. She wagged a finger at Maddie. "I shall see you again, my dear!" She clapped her hands. "Cat! Come!" she commanded, turning and walking away.

Sorrel gave her a highly indignant look.

"Cat!" Ionie said more insistently. "Come!"

Sorrel flounced down the steps.

"Well," Maia heard Maddie's mum say, "what a peculiar woman. If she comes to the door again, make sure you call me straight away next time."

Maddie nodded, and they went inside.

Sorrel bounded in through the willow branches, followed a few minutes later by Ionie.

"*Cat, come?*" Sorrel exclaimed, glaring at Ionie as she transformed back into her usual self.

"Sorry, Sorrel!" Ionie spread her hands. "I was in character."

"*Hrrumph!*" Sorrel snorted and turned her back on her, the end of her tail twitching angrily.

Ionie went over and stroked her. "I really am sorry. I won't talk to you like that again."

"I should think not," said Sorrel tartly but she gave Ionie's hand a lick with her small pink tongue. "I will forgive you this time. You excelled yourself and shown you have so much talent with magic. I have taught you well." She purred proudly.

"Did you find out if Maddie's a Star Friend?" Lottie asked.

"No, but she did say she believed in magic," said Ionie.

"And I could smell that a Star Animal had been close to Maddie's front door," said Sorrel. "It was the same scent that we found by the stream."

"She's got to be the otter's Star Friend!" said Maia triumphantly.

"Yay! We can tell her about Star Magic, and she'll start hanging round with us. Brilliant!" Lottie said.

"No, no, no," said Sorrel sharply. "Just because

I smelled that a Star Animal had been in the front garden doesn't mean the girl who lives there is definitely a Star Friend. The animal could have been going to one of the other houses in the street. We need absolute proof before anyone mentions Star Magic to her." Sorrel looked round at them. "Do you all understand?"

"Yes," they sighed. "We do."

☆★☆

"Oh, Bracken, I really want Maddie to be a Star Friend," Maia said when she got into bed that night. She'd told him everything that had happened.

He jumped up on to her bed and sat at the end. "I know you do but if Maddie's not the otter's Star Friend then I'm sure whoever is will be nice. Star Friends always are – they believe in magic, and they like to be kind and help people."

"I know. I just really want it to be Maddie," said Maia.

"Why?" asked Bracken curiously.

"Because then she'll like us more than anyone else," said Maia. She smiled happily as she imagined how amazing that would be. Her gaze fell on the mirror beside her bed. "You know what? I think I'll check up on her with magic. I might see her with the otter, and then we'll know for sure."

Bracken looked concerned. "Yesterday you said it didn't feel right to spy on her."

"I'll just take a quick peek," said Maia, picking up her mirror.

"I'm not sure you should, Maia," Bracken said uneasily.

But Maia ignored him. The urge to see Maddie was just too strong. "Show me what Maddie's doing," she said, cradling the mirror in her hands.

In its surface a picture of Maddie appeared. To Maia's disappointment, she wasn't with the Star Otter, but sitting in bed with her laptop and, just like in Maia's dream the night before, she seemed to be reading something off the screen and drawing pictures in the air.

"The otter's not there," Maia sighed.

"I think you should stop looking at her now," Bracken said. "You've seen she's not with the otter so put the mirror down."

"In a bit," said Maia, gazing at the picture. She wanted to keep watching. Maddie was so pretty and so nice.

I hope she hangs around with us in school tomorrow, she thought. *I hope she does science with us and eats lunch with us and…*

"Maia, I really think you should stop now." Bracken interrupted her thoughts.

"Oh, stop nagging me!" Maia snapped.

Her hands flew to her mouth as she saw the look of hurt cross Bracken's face. "Oh, Bracken," she said quickly, "I'm sorry. I didn't mean it!" She put down the mirror.

Bracken padded up the bed and climbed on to her lap. As Maia put her arms round him, her desire to see Maddie faded away, and she felt a stab of guilt. She couldn't believe she'd just snapped at him like that. "I'm sorry. I really am."

His indigo eyes were serious for once. "Something doesn't feel right. You're behaving strangely."

"I'm just tired," said Maia. "I think it's because I've had such vivid dreams the last two nights."

Bracken didn't look convinced.

She turned the light off and lay down. He cuddled up next to her, and she stroked his soft fur.

But, as she drifted off to sleep, Maia couldn't help but think about what he'd said. Was she behaving oddly? She'd felt such a strong desire to see Maddie – she hadn't been able to resist it, even though she had decided that spying on her with magic was wrong. Maybe something *was* going on?

No, she thought sleepily. *Maddie's just so nice. It's not strange that I want to hang out with her all the time. Not strange at all.*

Chapter Seven

Maia's dreams that night were just as vivid as the previous two: the otter by the river; the bedroom she'd seen before with scarves on the walls; Maddie asleep in bed, one hand flung out and touching her bedside table with its jumble of objects; two girls shouting at each other; a group of their classmates arguing; someone being tripped up and crashing down on to the grass; a mob of people chasing after someone with dark hair in school uniform who looked like Maddie; then Maddie sitting beside a bramble bush, cuddling an animal.

Maia woke with a start and looked at her clock. Her heart sank. Her alarm was about to go off, and she didn't feel like she'd had any rest at all. What did all her dreams mean? And why had so many of them had Maddie in?

Bracken sat up, his fur ruffled. "Are you OK, Maia?"

"Mmm," she said.

She glanced at the mirror beside her bed but the urge she'd felt the night before to watch Maddie had faded. Maia couldn't believe she'd snapped at Bracken about it. She remembered how desperate she'd been to see Maddie. It seemed ridiculous now. Definitely not something to argue with Bracken about.

Maia remembered the dream she'd had about Maddie being chased – and a flicker of alarm ran through her. Was Maddie in some kind of danger?

I need to talk to the others, she decided. *I'll tell them about my dreams at school.*

But, when she did get there, she forgot all about telling her friends. Maddie was in the playground with people clustered round her – there was Tara, and Sadie, some of the boys, Amy, Shruti and Lucy as well as Elissa, Harriet and Anoushka, who'd shared a tent with Maddie at camp. They all seemed to be vying for her attention, talking over each other.

"So you're still coming shopping with us on Saturday?" Tara was saying to Maddie.

"But, Maddie, we want you to come to our riding stables on Saturday!" protested Amy.

"Elissa, Harriet and I are going to watch a movie," said Anoushka. "You could come with us, if you wanted."

Tara turned on her. "Maddie doesn't want to watch a movie with you! She's coming with us!"

"No, she's not!" Anoushka and Elissa shouted.

"She is!" Tara shouted back.

"No, she wants to come riding!" cried Amy.

Maddie put her hands to her head; she looked overwhelmed by the attention.

Maia elbowed her way past people until she was able to touch Maddie's arm. "Hey, Maddie. Are you OK?" She pulled her back out of the crowd. Everyone was so busy arguing about what Maddie was going to do on Saturday that they didn't even notice.

Maia led Maddie round the side of the building where people couldn't see them so easily. "Wow, they all really want you to do stuff with them on Saturday, don't they?" She grinned. "What have you done? Cast a spell on them?"

Maddie's face paled. "What?"

"I was just joking," said Maia quickly.

"Maia, do you believe in spells?" Maddie said, her voice suddenly urgent.

"Um…" Maia didn't know what to say.

Maddie shook her head. "Oh, it doesn't matter." She sighed. "What am I going to do? I really want to go and see the riding stables with Amy, Lucy and Shruti, but I don't want to upset the others."

Maia peered out from behind the wall of the building. A full-scale argument was going on in the playground. "I think it might be a bit late for that." She looked back at Maddie. She liked it being just the two of them. "You could always come round to my house."

Maddie gave her a small smile. "Thanks, but it doesn't really help with the not-wanting-to-upset-anyone thing."

The bell rang. They waited until everyone had lined up and then hurried across the playground to join the end of their class's line. Ionie was there. Maia wondered if she'd ask her where she'd been and why she hadn't met up with her, Sita and Lottie like she usually did, but Ionie was too busy smiling at Maddie.

"Maddie!" she said, flinging her arms round her.

Maddie blinked. "Oh, hi, Ionie."

Maia stared in surprise. Ionie almost never hugged anyone.

Other people in the line had realized she was there and started to cluster round her. "Hey, Maddie!"

"Maddie!"

"Where did you disappear to?"

Even the people in Sita and Lottie's class started to join in.

"Year Six!" Mrs King, the headteacher, shouted. "What are you doing? Get back in line immediately!"

Reluctantly, everyone did as they were told and they all trooped inside.

★ ★ ★

Maddie-mania continued all day. In science, everyone wanted Maddie to be their partner, and Miss Amadi had to shout at them to calm down. Maddie chose to go with Maia and Ionie again. They were both delighted.

After lunch, they had a final practice for sports day with Nick the coach. The arguing started again.

"Maddie, don't go with that team – come with us!" Harriet called when Maddie joined Amy, Lucy and Shruti.

"No, come with us," said Tara, beckoning her over to where she was in a group with Sadie and two other girls.

"Tara, you're already in a four," said Nick.

"Well, Sadie can go with someone else," said Tara, giving Sadie a shove.

"Hey!" Sadie protested, pushing her back.

"Please don't fight, I don't like it," said

Maddie, looking alarmed.

"You're upsetting Maddie!" shouted Elissa. "Stop it!"

"Girls!" said Nick. "That's enough. The teams for the fun events are staying as they are."

Amy, Lucy and Shruti beamed and linked arms with Maddie. But everyone else seemed very unhappy and, when it came to practising the fun races, someone tripped Lucy up so she hurt her ankle.

Miss Amadi had been watching from the classroom and came running over to the field, looking very worried. "Lucy, are you all right?"

"It really hurts," said Lucy, her face pale.

"Let me see." Miss Amadi gently examined it, frowning in concentration. "I think it's just twisted," she said after a few minutes. "I'll put some ice on it and elevate it. I'm sure it'll feel better soon."

Lucy wiggled it tentatively. "It's feeling better already. But can Maddie come down to the classroom with me and keep me company?"

"Yes, of course," said Miss Amadi. "Come on, Maddie."

Maddie and Miss Amadi helped Lucy hobble back to the classroom. Maia watched them go. It wasn't fair. She wanted to be with Maddie, too.

"I'll go with them," she volunteered.

"And me!" said Ionie and most of the rest of the group.

"No!" said Nick firmly. "You're going to stay here and finish the practice."

Grumbling and muttering unhappily, everyone did as he said.

"I hate this," said Ionie at the end of school. In the cloakroom, a crowd of people were gathering round Maddie, asking her if she wanted to go back to their house for tea. "I want Maddie to be our friend."

"Me too," Maia agreed. "We really need to think of another way to find out if she's a you-know-what." She didn't say Star Friend because there were too many people around. "If she is, then she'll have to be best friends with us."

"Why don't you ask if you can come over to my house now?" said Ionie. "We can go to the clearing and think up a plan!"

★★☆

On the way to the clearing, they stopped at the Copper Kettle café. Maia's mum had given her some money to buy everyone an ice cream. Mary, who owned the Copper Kettle, made the best ice cream. The girls now knew it was extra delicious because it contained a tiny little bit of magic, but that was their and Mary's secret. They'd helped her out when she'd tried adding a magic charm to her cakes, too, and made them so popular that people had even started breaking into the café.

As Maia licked her honeycomb-crunch ice cream and waited for the others to choose theirs, she looked round the cosy café. There were mismatched comfy chairs at the tables and shelves filled with antique dolls and teddies. The walls were covered with old posters in frames. In the winter, a fire was usually burning in the fireplace but in the summer months it was home to an old copper kettle full of dried flowers.

Maia thought back to the afternoon they had found the café crammed with people demanding that Mary give them cake. Maia had eaten some of the magic cakes, too, and could vividly remember how they'd made her feel – at the time, she had felt as if nothing in the world mattered apart from Mary's cakes. They were all Maia could think about, all she wanted to eat. She'd even dreamed about them.

Something flickered across her mind. Wasn't that a little bit like how she was feeling now about Maddie? She was thinking about her, dreaming about her. Nothing felt as important as being her friend, and Maia clearly wasn't the only person who felt that way…

A picture of Maddie that morning swam into her head, her blue eyes wide and worried as they'd hidden round the side of the building. "*Do you believe in spells?*" she'd said.

Maia caught her breath.

Oh no, no, no. Could Maddie be doing magic?

Chapter Eight

"You think Maddie's doing magic to make people like her?" said Lottie in astonishment as they went down the lane. The moment they'd left the Copper Kettle, Maia had told them what she'd been thinking.

"Not Maddie!" said Ionie, shaking her head. "She'd never do anything bad."

"She wouldn't put a spell on us. I know she wouldn't," said Sita.

Part of Maia felt exactly the same but she remembered what Bracken had said to her the night before. "Bracken thinks I'm acting oddly."

"Sorrel said that about me, too," Ionie admitted.

"And Willow told me that she thought something might be going on," said Sita.

"Juniper said that to me as well," said Lottie, looking at them. "I guess it is kind of weird how everyone suddenly wants to be Maddie's friend."

"Is it?" said Sita. "She's so nice."

"Who wouldn't want to be her friend?" said Ionie.

"Yeah, actually it does make sense," said Lottie. "Of course people are fighting over her."

Maia started to agree with them but then with a massive effort stopped herself. "No!" she said. "We're being affected again by whatever's going on. The animals are right: we're not behaving normally. We need to see them. When I was under the spell of Mary's cakes, stroking Bracken helped me fight against the urge. It made it fade." She broke into a run. "*Come on!*"

★★☆

As soon as they reached the clearing, they called their animals. Maia crouched down and gathered Bracken into her arms. He snuggled against her, twisting his head round so he could lick her chin. "I'm so glad to see you," she said.

"Is everything all right?" said Bracken.

"Not really." Holding him, Maia could feel the effects of the charm or spell or whatever it was starting to fade slightly. "You were right. Something's definitely up."

They all cuddled their animals and told them about how everyone – including themselves – was suddenly desperate to be friends with Maddie.

"It was weird at school," said Lottie. "People were fighting over who she should go with for sports day and what she should do on Saturday."

"I can't believe we didn't realize it was weird," said Ionie, stroking Sorrel. "But it felt perfectly normal." She shook her head. "I even hugged her!"

"It definitely sounds like this girl is using magic!" said Sorrel.

"But what about the Star Otter and Maddie being its Star Friend?" said Sita.

"Could she have done something like this with Star Magic?" Maia said to Bracken.

"No," said Bracken. "Star Magic can't change the way other people think and feel in this way. Though, while you were at school, I did feel my fur tingle, almost like someone was using Star Magic nearby."

"Me too," said Juniper.

"Well, it's definitely not Star Magic that this girl is using," said Sorrel. "So what is it?"

"And how do we stop her?" said Ionie.

"Let's go round to her house and talk to her," said Maia.

"Good plan," said Ionie, jumping to her feet.

"Wait!" said Lottie. "If we do, won't we just be affected by the magic again?"

Maia thought quickly. "We have to go with our Star Animals, and after we've finished talking to Maddie, Sita can use her magic to command her to forget she's seen them."

"Do we have to do that?" said Sita anxiously. "I don't like commanding people."

"I might have another idea," said Bracken. "Does anyone know much about defensive shields – the ones Maia can make?"

The other three animals shook their heads.

"I think I can remember being told by one of the older animals in the Star World that they can be used to protect Star Friends against spells and charms," said Bracken.

"How?" said Maia.

"I'm not completely sure," Bracken admitted. "But it was something to do with pulling the shield tighter and tighter until it covers you like an invisible skin."

"I'll have a go," said Maia eagerly.

Taking a deep breath, she opened her mind to the magic current and imagined it forming a protective bubble round her and the others. The air shimmered as a shield formed. Maia focused on it and tried to pull it closer with her mind. She could feel it slowly shrinking, getting smaller and smaller, but it was hard work. Although she wasn't moving, she felt as if every cell in her body was straining, her heart beating faster, her breath coming more quickly. The shield trembled and then suddenly burst with a pop.

"I almost had it," she panted. "It's hard to do though."

"How about if we all help?" said Sita. "That's worked before when you've needed a shield to be strong."

"Try it," said Willow. "When you work together and all draw on the current, you increase your power."

They took hold of each other's hands. "After three," Maia said. "One… Two… Three!"

They connected to the magic current and now, instead of it just tingling through her from her head to her toes, Maia could feel it surging and rushing through her. It was like the difference between a little stream trickling down a mountainside and a huge river crashing over a waterfall. She focused on controlling the power and using it. The shield appeared again.

Shrink. Shrink, Maia thought, shutting her eyes
and pulling the barrier closer with her mind. It
was getting smaller and smaller. It was touching
them now. Maia felt a resistance but she kept
pulling and pulling until suddenly something
seemed to release, like a blockage being washed
away. A wave of energy spread over her, her

whole body tingled and then the sensation faded.

She opened her eyes. "Did you feel that?"

The others nodded. "It was weird," said Lottie. Letting go of Maia's hand, she lifted her arm. As she moved it upwards, it left just a faint shimmer in the air. "Look!" Lottie said.

Maia tried, and her arm did the same thing. She wiggled her fingers and the air shimmered around them.

"I think you've done it, Maia," said Bracken excitedly. "The shield is now protecting you all, which means you'll be immune to any kind of magic that tries to change the way you feel or think."

"That was a very clever idea, fox," said Sorrel, sounding surprised. "For once."

"How long will the shield last?" Sita asked.

"I don't know," said Bracken.

"Let's go to Maddie's now then, while it's working," said Maia.

They hugged their animals goodbye and left.

Ionie wanted to shadow-travel there but Sita pointed out it would be hard to explain it to Maddie if they just suddenly appeared in her house.

As they ran back up the lane, they passed Miss Amadi, who was out for a walk. She looked deep in thought, but she smiled when she saw them. "Hi, girls. Have you been on the beach?"

"In the woods," Maia said.

"That's where I'm going now," said Miss Amadi. "I'll see you tomorrow."

They said goodbye and hurried on.

When they turned on to Brook Street, they skidded to a halt. Outside Maddie's house there was a crowd of Year Six girls. Some of them were knocking on Maddie's door; others were arguing. Maia could hear them from where they were standing.

"Maddie doesn't want to be in your team for sports day. She wants to be with me!"

"No, she doesn't. I'm her best friend!"

"Maddie's with us. She likes ponies same as us and Nick said no swapping teams!"

"She's not going to be with you! She's not!" The arguing girls started to push each other.

"Maddie! Maddie!" other people shouted.

"How do we get past everyone?" said Sita.

"I could use my magic and climb up to her bedroom," said Lottie, looking at a creeper growing up the wall of the house.

"Not with everyone watching," said Sita.

"I know!" Ionie said suddenly. "I'll make everyone follow me, and you can get to Maddie."

"How will you do that?" said Maia.

Ionie checked no one was looking at them and then transformed into Maddie. "Ta-da!" she said with a grin.

Maia, Lottie and Sita gaped at Ionie.

"What are you doing?" Lottie said.

Maia guessed what was in Ionie's mind. "No, Ionie, it's too dangerous!" She went to grab Ionie's arm but she was already jogging down the road towards the arguing crowd.

"Hey, guys!" she shouted in a voice just like Maddie's. She waved her arms. "Over here!"

Everyone swung round.

"Maddie!" they all shrieked.

Ionie raced back past Maia, Sita and Lottie. "Make sure there are some shadows in the bedroom!" she gasped as she shot past them with the crowd in hot pursuit.

CHAPTER NINE

"What's Ionie doing? They're bound to catch her!" said Lottie in alarm.

"They won't," said Maia, suddenly realizing what Ionie's words had meant. "I think she's planning to lead them all away from here, and then she'll jump into a patch of shadows and disappear, reappearing in Maddie's bedroom." She looked at Maddie's house. "Which means we've got to get in there fast!"

They ran to the front door. Maia lifted the letterflap. "Maddie! It's me – Maia!" she called.

"With Sita and Lottie."

Nothing happened.

"Maybe she's not inside," said Sita.

Maia glanced up at the upstairs windows. She was sure she could see someone standing there. "I think she is."

She tried again. "Maddie, please. It's just us!" she called through the letterbox. "Everyone else has gone. Let us in. We can help you. We know about magic!"

"Maia!" hissed Lottie in alarm.

"We don't need to tell her about Star Magic," whispered Maia.

There was the sound of footsteps on the stairs, and then the door opened a crack. Maddie peered round it. Her face was pale, her eyes scared. "Do you really know about magic?" she said.

"Yes!" said Maia. "And we can help you."

Maddie opened the door wide, and they hurried in. She shut it and locked it behind them. "Did you see everyone from school out there? It was so scary! I thought they were going to break in."

"Where's your mum or your dad?" asked Lottie.

"My dad doesn't live with us. Mum had to go out to post a letter. She'd just gone when everyone turned up." Tears welled in Maddie's eyes, and she slumped down on the bottom step of the staircase. "I didn't mean for this to happen when I did the magic! It's all gone wrong!" She buried her face in her hands and started to cry.

Sita sat beside her. "It's OK," she said softly, putting her hand on Maddie's back. "It's all going to be fine. We'll help you sort it out."

She spoke soothingly, stroking Maddie's back. Maia realized she was using her magic ability to comfort and calm people. Maddie's tears dried up and she gave Sita a hopeful look.

"Do you really think you can sort this out?"

"I'm sure we can," said Sita. "Why don't we go to your room, and you can tell us what's been going on?"

Maddie led the way up to her bedroom and sat down on the bed. "I just wanted to make friends," she said. "I wanted everyone to like me, and it seemed to be working at first, but now they've all gone crazy, and I can't be with the people I really like, like you lot and Amy, Lucy and Shruti. And look." She took a crumpled piece of paper out of her pocket and showed it to them. "Someone pushed this through the letterbox." There was a message written on it.

If you don't swap teams for sports day, then you'll be sorry — and so will Shruti, Amy and Lucy!

Maddie gave them a despairing look. "I don't know what to do."

"What kind of magic did you do?" Maia asked.

In reply, Maddie got up, went to her desk and opened her laptop. She clicked on a tab, and a website popped up. Maia saw that it was the same website she had seen on Maddie's screen before. At the top it said:

So you want people to like you? This is what to do...

Maia joined Maddie at the desk. Up close, she could see that underneath the title there were the words:

A spell to bring you popularity.

And then there were a load of words to recite and some pictures of shapes.

"I've always believed in magic, and I like to read about it – mainly on the internet," said Maddie. "I found this site the other day. It says that before you go to sleep you have to say the spell and draw the runes in the air – the pictures on the page. I did it, and the next morning the spell began to work. People started wanting to be my friend."

Maia looked at the others. At least they knew what had happened now but she didn't have a clue how they would put it right. She didn't know anything about spells or runes. None of them did.

"What should I do?" Maddie asked.

"We can help you," said Lottie to Maia's

surprise. "But we'll need some things — a bowl of water, some salt, and have you got any herbs in your garden?"

"Mum has some pots of mint and thyme and rosemary in the back garden," said Maddie.

"Great, we'll need twenty leaves from each of those plants," said Lottie. "Exactly twenty. Count them carefully."

Maddie nodded. "OK." She left.

Maia turned to Lottie. "So you know how to stop the spell?"

"No," said Lottie. "I just wanted to get her out of here for a little while so we can call the animals and see what they think!"

Despite her worry, Maia grinned. They called their animals' names. At the same time as the animals appeared, there was a clatter from the side of the wardrobe, and Ionie stepped out of the shadows between the wardrobe and the wall, knocking over a pair of riding boots. She looked a bit out of breath, but her green eyes were shining.

"I got away from them! I thought they were going to catch me at one point, but then I found some shadows. Phew!"

"What's going on, Maia?" said Bracken, putting his front paws on her legs.

Seeing Bracken, Juniper and Willow, Ionie quickly called Sorrel.

"Yeah, what is going on?" she said as the wildcat appeared.

With Lottie keeping watch at the door, Maia quickly explained. "The spell Maddie did is there on the laptop."

Sorrel jumped up on to Maddie's chair and peered at the screen. "It's not magic," she said after a moment.

Maia frowned. "But it's got to be."

"Yes, Maddie said that the magic started working the day after she did it," said Sita.

"Well, whatever's happening is not because of this spell," said Sorrel with a sniff. "There's no magic in these words at all."

Maia stared. "If it's not the spell that's making Maddie popular, then what is?"

Willow sniffed the air. "You know, I think I can smell something magic in here somewhere." Lowering her head, she walked over to the bedside table. "It's near here." She sniffed the objects and then suddenly pulled back, her ears pricking.

"There!" she said. "The brown bottle. It's definitely magic!"

"This?" said Maia, picking up the perfume bottle. "But it can't be. Maddie and I made our perfumes using the same oils." She pulled her own identical perfume bottle from her pocket and held it out. "If hers is magic, then mine must be, too."

Willow sniffed Maia's perfume bottle. "Yours

doesn't smell of magic," she said. "But Maddie's definitely does."

"But how can that have happened?" said Maia.

"Right now, how it happened isn't important," said Sorrel. "We need to get rid of this perfume before the girl comes back."

"I know! Let's swap the bottles!" said Bracken. "Maia, you take the perfume with the magic in and leave yours for Maddie."

"Brilliant idea!" Maia said. She quickly swapped the labels on the two perfume bottles and put hers on the bedside table. "Now we can work out what to do with this!" she said, holding up Maddie's perfume.

"She's coming up the stairs," hissed Lottie, shutting the door. "What should we do? She's expecting a spell to reverse the one she did."

Ionie's face lit up. "I think Psychic Sue can help with that!" She transformed into the fortune-teller.

"Ionie!" gasped Lottie. "How are we going

to explain…"

The door handle turned, and Maddie came in, carrying a bowl of water and the other things Lottie had asked for. Lottie broke off, and the animals vanished.

"OK, I've got everything," Maddie said. "I…" She gave a startled squeak as she saw Ionie/Psychic Susan. "How did she get in here?" she exclaimed.

CHAPTER TEN

Lottie hastily took the bowl of water before Maddie dropped it in shock.

"Everything's OK," Sita said reassuringly, putting her hand on Maddie's arm. "Psychic Susan is a friend of ours. She's come to help. You mustn't worry about it."

Maia saw Maddie's shoulders relax as Sita's soothing magic worked. "Oh, OK. But … but how did she get up to my room?"

"Do not question the working of magic, my dear," said Ionie, wagging a finger at her

solemnly. Maia bit back a giggle. "I believe you
need a reversal spell."

"Y-yes," stammered Maddie.

"Then set forth the ingredients that you
were commanded to procure!" Ionie said
dramatically.

Maddie looked confused.

"She means the things I told you to get,"
Lottie translated.

"Oh." Maddie put everything on the bedside
table. "Here they are."

"Very good. Now I must warn you that the
magic I am about to perform is very powerful,"
Ionie told her in a solemn voice. "Very
powerful indeed."

"Really?" breathed Maddie.

Ionie nodded and waved her hand over the
water. Then she picked up the herbs and tossed
them in the bowl. Water splashed out on to the
bedside table. "Oops!" Ionie exclaimed in her
normal voice. She quickly covered it up with

a cough and carried on in her Psychic Susan voice. "Oopsy, woopsy, now magic revert!" she declared. "Before anyone gets badly hurt!"

She brandished the salt cellar like a waiter at a fancy restaurant, grinding the salt into the water.

"Recite the spell you used, my dear!" she commanded.

Maddie read out the words from the website then drew the pictures in the air with her finger. "That's it," she said as she finished.

Ionie clapped her hands. "And so the reverting spell is cast." She backed towards the wardrobe. "And it is time for Psychic Sue to leave at last!"

Stepping into the shadows, she vanished.

There was a moment of stunned silence.

"She disappeared!" Maddie squeaked, pointing to the shadows.

"Yeah, um, she just went … poof!" said Lottie.

"So she was properly magic," said Maddie, her eyes as round as saucers.

"Yes, but you mustn't tell anyone," said Maia. "It's got to be our secret."

Maddie nodded hard. "Do you think the magic really has stopped?"

"Yes," said Maia, thinking of the perfume bottle in her pocket. "Or at least it should be better by the morning."

She remembered how she had felt less affected by the perfume when she'd woken up that day – its magic must have started to wear off overnight and had only reactivated when she'd smelled it again. Hopefully the same would happen again, and by tomorrow everyone's Maddie-mania would be fading.

Maddie sighed. "I guess that means no one at school will like me any more."

"We will," said Sita, going over and giving her a hug.

"Yes, we'll still be your friends," said Lottie. "And then, in September, you and I are going to the same school so we'll be able to get the bus together, and we might even be in the same class!"

"And you seemed to be getting on really well with Shruti, Lucy and Amy today," said Maia. "I bet they'll still like you."

"I hope so," said Maddie. "I hadn't talked to them much before I did the spell but they're nice and really into ponies – just like me." She waved at one wall that was covered with pony posters. "Mum said she'll take me to the riding stables they go to and see if she can book me a lesson." She smiled. "Thanks for coming round and helping me."

They went downstairs.

"Maddie," Maia said suddenly as they reached the door, "you haven't seen an otter near here, have you?"

"An otter?" Maddie echoed. "No. Are there wild otters living round here then?"

Maia shrugged. "A friend just thought she'd seen one."

"Well, I'll keep my eyes open," said Maddie, opening the front door. "I really love otters. There was an otter sanctuary near my old house." She smiled. "That's where I got my otter ruler and poster."

They said goodbye and were just leaving the house when a parcel delivery man came up the path. "I've got a parcel for your neighbour at number twenty-two," he said. He read the label. "A Miss Ginika Amadi. She's not in."

"That's OK. You can leave it here," said Maddie.

She took the parcel and said goodbye to

Maia and the others.

As the door shut, Maia grabbed Lottie and Sita's arms. "Let's go to the weeping willow," she said.

As they hurried into their hiding place under the branches, they called their animals, and Maia took out her phone and texted Ionie to tell her where they were. A few seconds later, they were all there.

"Maddie's definitely not the Star Friend," said Maia. "She told us she hadn't seen an otter."

"And I didn't smell any hint of a Star Animal in her room," said Willow.

"I wonder who did something to her perfume and why?" said Lottie.

"Maia, can you use your magic to find out who it was?" asked Ionie.

Maia took her compact mirror out. "I can try."

She held the mirror in her hands. "Show me who changed Maddie's perfume into a magic potion," she said.

She held her breath as a picture appeared. What would it show?

The picture slowly became clear. "It's Miss Amadi!" Maia exclaimed. The magic showed their teacher opening Maddie's perfume bottle and squeezing three drops into it from another little bottle she'd taken out of her pocket.

"Miss Amadi? But why?" said Lottie, astonished. Maia didn't have a clue. Miss Amadi seemed so nice. Why would she have done something to Maddie's perfume?

"We have to talk to her and find out why she did it," said Ionie. "Can you use your magic to find out where she lives, Maia?"

"No need," said Maia. "She lives next door to Maddie at number twenty-two."

Ionie ducked out through the willow branches.

"Ionie! Wait!" Maia checked there was nothing coming then ran across the road after her, with Lottie and Sita following. "Miss Amadi's out," she said as Ionie knocked on the door. "We met a delivery man trying to drop a parcel off here."

"She's probably still walking in the woods," said Lottie.

Through the window by the front door, Maia could see into Miss Amadi's kitchen. There was something strangely familiar about it. A slow cooker was plugged in on the worktop next to some other appliances. Maia suddenly realized where she'd seen it before.

"This is the kitchen I dreamed about the other night!" she exclaimed.

"But why would your dreams show you

Miss Amadi's kitchen?" said Sita.

"I bet I know," said Ionie suddenly. "In our perfume lesson, she told us that she made her own essential oils at home. Well, maybe she doesn't just distil normal essential oils. Maybe she distils magical oils, and that's what she put in Maddie's perfume!"

"But I just don't get why she'd do that," said Sita.

They stared at each other.

"We have to find her!" said Lottie.

Maia took out her mirror. "Show me where Miss Amadi is," she said.

A picture appeared. It showed Miss Amadi sitting by the stream in the clearing talking to an otter with indigo eyes.

Maia's free hand flew to her mouth.

"What is it?" said Sita quickly.

Maia lowered the mirror and stared at her friends. "Miss Amadi is the Star Friend we've been looking for!"

Chapter Eleven

Maia described to the others what she could see with her magic. "She's with the Star Otter in the clearing right now!"

"But why would Miss Amadi use plant magic if she's a Star Friend?" said Lottie.

"There's one way to find out." Ionie made sure no one was around and held out her hands. "I'll shadow-travel us there, and we can ask her."

They all formed a circle. As they clasped hands, they felt the world rush away. Shadow-travelling was a very strange experience. For a moment, Maia felt as if she was floating, and then the ground zoomed back to meet her. She felt the thump against her feet and blinked her eyes open. They were in the shadows of the trees in the clearing.

Bracken, Willow, Juniper and Sorrel appeared beside them. Miss Amadi gasped as she saw them appear, and the otter vanished.

"It's OK, Miss Amadi," said Ionie, stepping forward. "Your Star Animal can come back."

"We're Star Friends, too," Maia added.

Miss Amadi gaped. "You're all Star Friends?" she said in astonishment.

They nodded.

The otter reappeared beside her. "We've never met any other Star Friends," she said, her voice soft as she gazed at the girls and their animals.

"Did you meet each other at camp?" Ionie asked.

"At camp?" echoed Miss Amadi. "No, I met Fen when I was twelve. I've been her Star Friend ever since." The otter put her paws on her knee and nuzzled her cheek.

Maia blinked in surprise. "But, if you've been together that long, why haven't our animals felt you doing any Star Magic?"

"I hardly ever use Star Magic. Fen and I don't really know how to use the magic current properly," Miss Amadi said, stroking the otter. "I can sometimes connect to it and, when I do, I seem to be able to make people feel calmer or make them better if they're hurt. I helped Lucy this afternoon when she injured her ankle."

"That must have been when we felt Star Magic being used," said Bracken excitedly.

Miss Amadi shook her head wonderingly. "This is all so strange."

Maia crossed the clearing with Bracken beside her. "Have you really never met any other Star Friends?" She couldn't imagine what that would be like.

"No, I mean, I guess I may have met some over the years but, if I did, I never knew about it. My family moved around a lot when I was younger, and I never stayed anywhere long enough to find out if there were Star Friends there."

"And I travelled here from the Star World on my own," said Fen. "I was very young when I made the journey, and I don't know much about magic. You're the first Star Animals I've seen in the human world," she said to Bracken, Sorrel, Willow and Juniper.

Willow stepped forward and gently touched Fen's nose with her own. "It's good to meet you, Fen. I'm Willow." She nodded to the other animals one at a time. "And this is Juniper, Bracken and Sorrel."

Juniper leaped off Lottie's shoulder and scampered up on to the rocks near where Miss Amadi was sat. Fen joined him.

"We'll be your friends now, Fen!" Juniper said, his whiskers quivering.

"We'll help you learn all about Star Magic," said Bracken, trotting over. "Well, everything we know or have worked out so far."

Sorrel was the only animal who hung back. She looked from Fen to Miss Amadi. "Why did you cause so many problems with the perfume?" she said. "Star Friends should help people, not bring trouble. Even if you don't know much about Star Magic, surely you must know that?"

A guilty look crossed Miss Amadi's face. "Oh, the perfume. I've been feeling awful about that all day." Fen nuzzled her hand. "I only wanted to help Maddie. She seemed so lonely. I just wanted to give her a helping hand with making friends. I added three drops of gbajumo oil to her perfume when the class were out practising for sports day. I learned about it from my aunt. She uses plant magic to help people, and she taught me how to get magic essences from plants. The gbajumo plant can be used to attract people – it makes others want to be your friend. I think I used too much though."

She shook her head. "I never meant for things to get so out of hand and for people to react the way they did. I came here to meet Fen to try to work out how to get the perfume off Maddie. If she stops using it, the effects should fade quite quickly."

"But we haven't thought of a way to do that yet," said Fen.

"Don't worry," said Maia, pulling the bottle out of her pocket. "This is Maddie's perfume." She handed it to Miss Amadi, who stared at it in astonishment.

"How did you get this?"

"It's a long story," said Maia. "The important thing is that Maddie hasn't got it any more."

"So you know how to do plant magic?" Ionie said to Miss Amadi.

"Yes. When I became Fen's Star Friend and found out that magic was real, I set out to learn all I could about it. I use what I know to help people and make life better for them. My aunt taught me about plant magic, and I've collected objects with many magic properties as I've travelled round the world. I've also learned a bit about how to use crystal magic…"

"The raccoon!" Maia burst out, remembering the magic showing her a dark-haired girl or woman placing the pottery raccoon with a pink crystal acorn in Mrs Coates's porch. "Were you the person who left it for Mrs Coates when we were at camp?"

"Yes," said Miss Amadi. "The crystal in its paws turns negative energy into positive energy – it changes anger to happiness; unfriendliness to friendliness. I knew Mrs Coates was very unhappy about the camp being next to her farm, and so I put the raccoon with the crystal in her porch. I wanted to help."

"But then she brought the raccoon back," said Maia, remembering the farmer stomping into camp with it on the first night.

Miss Amadi smiled. "Yes, so I took it back again. Do you remember? I gave it back to her when I dropped off the chicken toys we'd made for her hens."

"And, by the next night, the magic had worked, and she was friendly," said Maia.

Miss Amadi nodded. "It's still working," she

said. "Connie from camp told me yesterday that Mrs Coates is now a big fan of the campers."

"Wait! Did you know about the Jeniyan Spirit being in the monkey as well?" said Ionie.

Miss Amadi bit her lip. "Yes, and that attempt at helping didn't go so well. I wanted it to make sure you were happy at camp, Ionie – you seemed so worried on the first day…"

"It wasn't *my* Star Magic that woke the Jeniyan Spirit up – it was *yours*!" Ionie realized.

"Yes. I told it to make sure you had a good time. Unfortunately, I didn't realize quite what it would do."

"Why didn't you try to stop it?" asked Lottie.

"I only realized it was the Jeniyan who was doing all the bad stuff around camp on the last day," said Miss Amadi. "And then it suddenly stopped. The spirit vanished. I couldn't understand it." Her eyes scanned their faces. "But now I'm guessing that had something to do with you?"

They all nodded.

"I sent it back to the Realm of Light," said Ionie.

"I can hardly believe this," said Miss Amadi. "The four of you. All Star Friends. And I didn't have a clue!"

Sita sat down beside her. "Now that you know, we'll be able to help you learn about Star Magic," she said. "And our animals will help Fen."

All the animals – even Sorrel – nodded.

"Thank you," Miss Amadi said, smiling.

"I really do want to learn how to use Star Magic to help people. Trying to use other types of magic has got me into all kinds of trouble – something nearly always seems to go wrong."

"Well, learning together is lots of fun!" said Juniper.

Bracken gave a cheeky bow. "And so's playing together!" He bounced at Fen and bopped her and Juniper gently with his nose. "Tag! You're both it!" He bounded away across the clearing with Willow cantering beside him.

Sorrel hesitated for a moment but, as Juniper scampered towards her, her eyes sparkled, and she streaked away.

She jumped on to a tree trunk and raced up it with Juniper following while Fen chased Willow and Bracken through the poppies and daisies, sending butterflies scattering into the sky. Maia felt her heart swell with happiness as she watched them. They'd solved the mystery and found another Star Friend. She glanced at Miss Amadi.

I'm glad she doesn't have to be on her own any more, Maia thought. *And Maddie, too. She might not have a magic perfume, but that doesn't matter. We'll still be friends with her, and I'm sure other people will, as well, now they know her better.*

"I wonder what will happen at sports day tomorrow," said Lottie. "Do you think the perfume will have worn off?"

"I hope so but we'll just have to wait and see!" said Miss Amadi.

☆★☆

To their relief, when they went into school the next day, people were behaving much more normally. Everyone seemed friendly with Maddie but there was no more arguing about whose team she was going to be on or what she was going to do at the weekend.

During sports day itself, she seemed to be having a great time with Shruti, Lucy and Amy. Afterwards she ran over to Maia and the others and told them she had arranged to go to the riding stables on Saturday. "They all help out there and I'm going to ask if I can too," she said happily. "I'll be able to muck out stables!"

"Sounds ... um ... fun," said Maia.

Maddie grinned. "It will be. I love doing anything with ponies." She turned to Lottie. "Oh, and Lottie, my mum wants to know if you'd like a lift to the High School induction day next week. We could go in together – if you want to, of course?" she added slightly shyly.

"I definitely do!" said Lottie, smiling at her.

"Great!" said Maddie, then she hurried off to join her mum, who had come to watch the competition.

"I wish Maddie was a Star Friend," Lottie whispered, watching her.

A picture flickered in Maia's head – Maddie cuddling an animal beside a bramble bush, an image she'd seen in her dreams. She'd thought she'd been seeing Maddie with a Star Otter but now she knew that couldn't be right. So, why had her dreams shown her Maddie with an animal? She frowned. Could it have been a glimpse into the future?

"Should we ask our mums and dads if we can go to the Copper Kettle on the way home?" Sita said, interrupting her thoughts.

"Oh, yes, let's," said Lottie.

Ionie linked arms with Maia. "We definitely deserve ice cream even though we didn't win. Come on!"

Maia pushed the image of Maddie with an

animal to the back of her mind and let Ionie
pull her away.

✩★✩

"I still can't believe we didn't win the team
competition," said Ionie a little while later as they
walked down the lane, finishing the ice creams
they'd bought from the Copper Kettle. "One
point!" she said. "Just one point!" In the end,
they'd come second to Jake, Tyler and Brad.

"I don't care," said Sita, linking arms with
her. "It was so much fun."

"And it was really good that the perfume
had worn off," said Lottie.

"I'm pleased that Maddie is friends with
Shruti, Lucy and Amy now," said Maia.

"As well as us," added Lottie.

"I guess it means the magic wasn't actually
a complete disaster," said Ionie. "It helped
Maddie make friends."

"You know what I think?" Maia said.

"What?" the others said.

She grinned at them. "Having friends is the best thing in the world! Race you to the clearing!"

She charged down the lane with the others hot on her heels. Pushing through the tall cow parsley on the footpath, they all burst into the sunny clearing and called their animals' names.

Bracken appeared and took a flying leap into Maia's arms. She buried her face in his soft fur, feeling happiness flood through her. They'd solved the mystery, they'd made people happy, and now there were end-of-term events to look forward to. Then they had the long summer holidays stretching out before them – sunny days filled with friends and magic.

"Oh, Bracken," she said, "we're going to have so much fun together!"

His eyes shone. "We always do!"

Star Friends

Dream Shield

Turn the page for
a sneak peek of
the Star Friends'
next adventure!

Coming soon...

In the Star World

Three wise animals — a wolf, a badger and a
stag — touched noses as they gathered round
a pool in the forest. Their fur glittered with
stardust. Around them, silvery trees reached
up towards the inky-black sky. Hearing a soft
hoot, the animals looked up to see a pale shape
gliding towards them. Hunter the owl landed
on a tree stump, his indigo eyes anxious.

"Thank you for meeting me here,
my friends. There is trouble brewing in
Westcombe. Someone close to the village has

been using dark magic to influence people for their own gain. This person is dangerous, and I am worried for our friends who live there."

The other animals exchanged uneasy looks.

Every so often, young creatures from the Star World travelled down to the human world to look for a child who believed in magic to be their Star Friend. After finding the right person, the animal stayed with them for life, teaching them how to connect to the magic current that linked the two worlds, helping them use it for good. Sometimes that meant assisting people with everyday problems, and at other times it meant stopping those who were using dark magic.

"Do our young friends in Westcombe know about the person who is using dark magic?" asked the badger.

"Not yet," replied Hunter. "So far this person has only used small amounts of magic to influence people, but their ambitions are growing. Our Star Friends and their Star Animals must stop them."

He swept a wing over the surface of a forest pool. The pool was a window to the human world and, as the animals watched, the glittering water swirled and an image appeared in it of four eleven-year-old girls and four animals in a clearing in a wood. The animals looked like regular woodland creatures apart from their deep indigo eyes.

"Maia and Bracken," said the wolf, her eyes moving first to a girl with shoulder-length dark blond hair who was tickling the fluffy tummy of a fox lying on his back.

"Sita and Willow," said the stag, his eyes resting on a girl with a thick brown plait and gentle eyes who was stroking a fallow deer. His gaze moved on to a girl with chin-length dark curly hair and hazel eyes who was giggling as a red squirrel jumped from one of her shoulders to the other. "Lottie and Juniper. And Ionie and Sorrel," she finished, looking at the girl with a strawberry-blond ponytail who had a tabby wildcat weaving through her legs.

"They have a lot of power between them," said the badger.

"They will need to use all their powers to stop the person who is using dark magic," said Hunter.

"Will it be dangerous?" asked the wolf anxiously.

Hunter nodded gravely. "I believe this will be the most dangerous challenge our young friends have faced yet."

ABOUT THE AUTHOR

Linda Chapman is the best-selling author of over 200 books. The biggest compliment Linda can have is for a child to tell her they became a reader after reading one of her books. Linda lives in a cottage with a tower in Leicestershire with her husband, three children, three dogs and three ponies. When she's not writing, Linda likes to ride, read and visit schools and libraries to talk to people about writing.

www.lindachapmanauthor.co.uk

ABOUT THE ILLUSTRATOR

Kim Barnes lives on the Isle of Wight with her partner and two children, Leo and Cameo, who greatly inspire her work. She graduated from Lincoln University, England, and has drawn ever since she was a young child.

www.kimmariaillustration.com